A Book For You

12 Questions to Free YourSelf from Yourself

By Stephen Parato

All Rights Reserved. No part of this publication may be reproduced in any form or by any means, including scanning, photocopying, or otherwise without prior written permission of the copyright holder.
Copyright Stephen Parato © 2019

Contents

Dedication
Preface
Chapter 1: Who Am I?
Chapter 2: Thoughts
Chapter 3: Emotions
Chapter 4: The "Real" You
Chapter 5: The Power of Choice
Chapter 6: Big Ship, Small Rudder
Chapter 7: Small Daily Steps
Chapter 8: Why Are You Here?
Chapter 9: Infinite Possibility
Chapter 10: Seeing Your New Life
Chapter 11: Upgrading Your Relationships
Chapter 12: You 2.0
Main Questions from Each Chapter
Practice Sheet
Spread the Love

Dedication

This book was conceived through an insatiable calling to inspire.... To spark something within YOU.

It's for anyone suffering. For anyone wrestling with their inner demons. For anyone experiencing pain, depression, anxiety, overwhelm, despair and hopelessness. For anyone who has wanted to just give up on life.

This is for YOU.

This is for every homeless person who, in their eyes, I saw myself.

This is for everyone recovering from trauma.

This is for everyone struggling with addiction, in any form.

This is for everyone who feels imprisoned, or might be physically imprisoned.

This is for anyone who feels like they've hit rock bottom.

This is for you.

This is the book I would've given myself at age 19, when I almost killed myself from alcohol poisoning.

Specifically, there are a few people I wish to acknowledge here.

Some of them have overcome enormous odds and grew into powerful beacons of light in this world. And all of them have inspired me on a deep, deep level.

The first is Mike Govoni. Mike went through one of the craziest childhoods I've heard of. And fell into addiction as a teenager. At age 21, he went into recovery and began his healing journey. A few years later though, he was diagnosed with several health problems, which he has healed naturally over the last few years.

Mike now works as a recovery coach and counselor in the Boston area, and is a shining example to people going through tough times. Thank you, Mike, for inspiring me and being a big inspiration for writing this book.

Then there's Zane Baker. Zane was born in Baghdad, Iraq. He grew up in a warzone, experiencing violence and horror on a daily basis. Zane ended up as a translator for the United States, and the officer who he was working for (the amazing Geoffrey Hand, who's also a dear friend) helped him migrate to the US and start a new life.

Since coming to the United States, Zane and Geoff started several businesses. Zane has also been on a journey of personal growth, healing his past and living the dream. Zane is one of the most loving, open-hearted people I've ever met.

Another notable inspiration for me is Seth Pruznanski. This guy experienced the rock bottom of addiction that most people never recover from. And he's risen to be an inspirational teacher and owner of two businesses.

Brandon Hawk has also inspired various parts of this book, through his profound work with emotional healing and radiant lightheartedness. It's no coincidence that Brandon released a book called "YOU" while I was writing this.

Jake Woodard is someone else who experienced extreme hardships in life, only to come out as a powerhouse transformation mentor, helping many other people overcome their obstacles.

Their life journeys amaze me. These are people I deeply admire, who are shining examples of human potential, and living proof that your past does not have to determine your future.

Then there's my mother and father, who throughout all of my ups and downs, were always there when I needed them. I am blessed and forever grateful.

My grandmothers too, who built wonderful families from scratch, when no one supported them.

And the biggest support system for me is my partner Nicole. She has shown me what real love is. She has held the space for me to look at the darkest parts of myself and let them heal. She is the reason I am able to write this in the first place.

Finally, there's YOU. This book is dedicated to YOU. Yes you, reading this right now.

I trust that this book sparks something for you.

This is A Book For You.

Wholeheartedly,
~ Stephen Parato

PS - Here's a list of more people who have inspired this book in some way...
- Bruce Lipton - For his work with beliefs and the subconscious mind
- Prince EA - For inspiring me to inspire more people
- Anik Singal - For insight into sustainable and empowering forms of charity work
- Steve Harrison - For ideas of how to simplify and frame the content of this book
- Sanaya Roman - For sharing potent, high-level spirituality with the world
- Ryan Holiday - For his approach to crafting deeply impactful, shareable writing
- Lao Tzu - For the eternal wisdom of the Tao Te Ching

- Michael Singer - For sparking my own self-inquiry process
- Eckhart Tolle - For bringing hope into my life when I felt hopeless
- Sevan Bomar - For activating my own innerstanding and sovereignty
- Martin Kenny - For sparking new worlds of thought and linguistic connections
- Bill Pulte - For continuous, creative giving through social media
- Dawson (Big Daws) - For making random acts of kindness funny and entertaining
- Annie Moniz - For reminding me to check my ego and serve from a pure place

Preface

This book is for you...

Why? Because we all need a little inspiration sometimes.

A little encouragement. A little boost. A little spark.

We've all seen what a little spark can do. It can lead to a chain reaction that creates something monumental. Remember, countless candles can be lit by one single candle.

This book is designed to help you become more of the real you, the best version of yourself, and completely upgrade your reality.

The questions posed here will help you free yourSelf from yourself. There are main questions for every chapter, as well as lots of other questions, that will spark some major aha moments for you.

There are no rules to follow. There's no assembly line process for you to go through. That's not how life works.

Life can be unpredictable. Life can be messy. Life can be chaotic. Life is full of curveballs and unpredictable storms. We get to turn those curve balls into home runs. We get to turn storms into opportunities to water our garden, while we're dancing in the rain.

There is no "controlled environment" in life. But that's also what makes it fun and worthwhile. If life were too predictable - too "safe" - it would be boring and unfulfilling.

Now, there's a balance... We all like a little spice in our lives, but no one wants to suffer. This book will help you turn suffering into challenges and challenges into the raw materials for building your best life. How are diamonds created? When coal experiences intense pressure. It's time to shine, baby.

You are just as worthy, powerful and special as everyone else. If you've forgotten that, or you're saying, "nope, not me", this book is your reminder.

I invite you to just give it a chance. Read with an open mind. What do you have to lose? And you never know… The one thing you dismiss might be the very thing that changes everything for you.

There's no fluff here. No philosophizing. Every concept here is directly applicable to your life right now.

I've used the lessons in this book to transcend alcoholism, porn addiction, debilitating anxiety, sugar addiction, narcissism, body dysmorphia, anger problems (there's probably more too, but I'll stop there). And on the other side of it, I'm still applying everything in this book, every single day, to step more and more into the best version of myself.

It goes way beyond me too. This book reverse-engineers some of the processes people I know went through to transcend poverty, addiction, trauma, depression and more.

Though this book isn't specifically about any of those situations, it applies to all of them. Whether it's overcoming addiction, getting healthier or building a business, the same personal qualities and meta-tools create success in each area.

Think of this as the "foundational awareness for total freedom and empowerment."

It's not intended to replace anything you're already doing. It's a new lens that you can use to enhance and amplify anything else you're doing. If you're in therapy, for example, this will add momentum and sustainability to your results.

Keeping all of this would be selfish, and a disservice to you. It needs to be shared. That's why this book is called, "A Book For You."

This book is the first step on your new journey. Take your time with it. There's no rush here. Don't overwhelm yourself. Allow this wisdom to integrate with grace and patience.

This is a portal for you to step into your new life.

You will see the world with new eyes. Doors will open up for you that you never would have expected. New worlds of possibility will be available to you.

Welcome to your new life.

Now let's begin...

Chapter 1: Who Am I?

Main Question:
Who Am I?

Who am I?

Have you ever really asked yourself this question?

Really, this should be the first question we explore in our lives. It's the foundation for everything, right?

How can you truly know anything if you don't know yourself?

If you don't know yourself, then everything else is based on distorted assumptions.

You're in this world, viewing it through a unique lens. Wouldn't it make sense to examine your lens? And wouldn't it make even more sense to know who is doing the viewing in the first place?

When people are feeling down and out, they might say something like this… "I can't live with myself." There's a subject ("I") and an object ("myself") in this sentence.

So who is the "I" that can't live with themselves? Well, that's what we're about to unveil…

When you speak of "I", who are you talking about?

When it comes to the question, "Who Am I?" it's most effective to simply ask the right questions…

Question #1: "Am I My Name?"

First of all, who is it that claims to have a name?

Let that question sink in…

That question, in and of itself, quickly reveals who you are not (in this case, your name). And it can be applied to all of the identities we cling to.

If you were to write down your name on a piece of paper, is that you? Of course not. You are not your name. Your name is just a label.

Just like the word "tree" isn't the actual tree, our name isn't our actual self. It's just a label. The truth of who we are cannot be confined to a label.

Question #2: "Am I A _____?"

Think about who you are in relation to society...

Are you a teacher? Are you a parent? Are you a brother or sister? Are you a mechanic? Are you a CEO? Are you a democrat? Are you an American? Are you a Christian?

Who is it that claims to be one of these? Who is it that claims to be a teacher, parent, American...etc?

Again, let that question sink in...

These are more labels. In this case, labels based on societal relationships.

Let's take a CEO as an example. A CEO is a job, a role, not who you are. So, who is playing the role of a CEO? Well we know it's not your name. We're getting closer to the truth...

Question #3: "Am I My Experiences?"

Who is it that's having experiences?

Let that one marinate...

You could list out all of your experiences, but that's definitely not you.

"You" were the experiencer of the experiences. So, who are you?

Who is experiencing the experiences?

We're getting closer...

Question #4: "Am I My Body?"

Who is it who claims to have a body?

Again, let that question sink in...

Your body is not you. We even say, "my body." So, who is it that has this body?

When someone dies, their body is still there, but "they" aren't there. So, you are not your body.

Question #5: "Am I My Thoughts?"

Here are two questions that can really shift your perspective...
1. "Who is the thinker of my thoughts?"
2. "Who is the observer of the thinker of my thoughts?"

Close your eyes, take a deep breath and ask those two questions to yourself. Don't try to answer them, just feel into it and let the questions integrate.

We have the ability to observe our thoughts. This is the basis of mindfulness. Simply observing thoughts.

Who is observing the thoughts?

Some people would say that their mind observes their thoughts. And they are their mind. Well, it depends on how you define mind.

If you define mind as your physical brain, that's not you. Because, as explored above, we are not our body. But what if you define mind as "awareness"?

We're getting really close now...

Question #6: "So, Who Am I?"

The only feasible answer to "Who am I?" is "I am."

What does this mean? Pure awareness.

What would life be like if your awareness didn't exist? "You" wouldn't exist!

The most accurate way of describing who we are is pure awareness. But don't get attached to that label. It's only a guidepost, not the real thing.

As Lao Tzu said, *"The Tao that can be spoken is not the eternal Tao."*

The truth of who you are, pure awareness, is beyond words. It is experiential.

Chapter 2: Thoughts

Main Question:
What Thoughts Am I Having Right Now?

We all know what thoughts are, but let's get clear here...

Here are a couple definitions of the word "thought":
- The product of mental activity
- A consideration of reflection

Now before we continue, I want to make this stuff experiential to you, not just concepts.

Stop reading for a moment, close your eyes, and observe your thoughts.

What's the first thought that popped into your head?

You can even write it down if you want, because writing makes your awareness even stronger.

If you pay attention, you'll realize that thoughts are circling around in your head constantly. And most of it is the same thoughts just looping over and over again. It's pretty crazy.

I remember the first time I tried to meditate. I "thought" I was crazy. I did the whole sit down cross-legged thing, and when I closed my eyes, it was a tsunami of chatter. My whole to-do list, what I wanted for dinner, what someone said to me in middle school…etc.

I then realized that this constant chatter was actually going on 24/7. But I was never even aware of it. It was an "aha moment" and a "wtf moment" all in one.

The Monkey Mind

The term "monkey mind" perfectly describes this. Our monkey mind is that aspect of our mind that's always chattering. It constantly re-hashes the past, obsesses about the future, and hangs onto trivial things.

If you ever catch yourself thinking about something over and over again, that's your monkey mind.

Yes, it can be helpful to learn from the past. Yes, it can be helpful to make plans for the future. But obsessing over it is when it becomes counterproductive to your life.

Constant mental chatter distracts you from the present moment. And the present moment is all we ever have. It's always now.

And guess what? When you're really in the present moment, it feels amazing. That's why it's the core of so many teachings and there are entire books written about presence.

Take a moment and feel into a time in your life when you were completely in the present moment.

It might have been watching a sunset, walking outside, having a great conversation, listening to birds chirping, making love, laughing...etc.

How did it feel? Pretty good, right?

In the absence of obsessive thoughts, we're fully in the moment, and it feels so good. Peace, serenity, joy, happiness, love and bliss are some of the most common feelings of being present.

Problems & The Present Moment

Pause...

And ask yourself: "Is there anything wrong with my life right now?"

Not 5 minutes ago. Not later today. At this very moment.

Feel what the present moment feels like.

"Problems" only exist in the past or future. Danger can be very real. But when you're truly in a dangerous situation, you don't have "time" to dwell on it as a "problem."

If you're running from a bear, it's not "good" or "bad." It doesn't "suck." You're just running, with no "time" to think about the past or future.

If you're reading this, you're not in immediate danger here and now. Yes, your "big picture situation" might not be ideal. But focusing on that doesn't change it. Bring your focus to this very moment, as you're reading this. This is all that exists right now, and it is your leverage point for your life.

So, take a couple deep breaths and be here now. Be present. Feel gratitude just for being alive in this moment. This space is your kingdom, where you reclaim your divine sovereignty.

Thoughts Have Power

Some people dismiss thoughts as inconsequential, with no real effect on reality.

Well, if thoughts had no power, then why does everything we see in society begin as a thought?

The airplane began as a thought. New York City began as a thought. The internet began as a thought.

Thoughts obviously have power, even though we can't explain the exact mechanics of it yet. Thoughts are the spark that initiates bringing things into the physical world.

You can feel thoughts too. Have you ever had someone direct really negative thoughts at you? You can feel the person stewing and throwing mental daggers. Have you ever had your mom or a relative worry about you? You can feel it, especially if you just pause and clear your own thoughts first.

Thoughts can be detected. And the more aware of your own thoughts you are, the sharper you become at detecting thoughts. It's both a superpower and something so simple at the same time.

Observation Leads to Change

The first step to changing anything is awareness.

In order to overcome addiction, you need to be fully aware that you're addicted. In order to lose weight, you need to be fully aware that it's possible and helpful for you to lose weight. This is common sense, right? Well, so many epiphanies come when you make the obvious become obvious.

Here's the cool thing with thoughts… Awareness, in and of itself, transforms thoughts.

It's true. I've seen this over and over again, within myself and so many other people.

When you bring full awareness to your thoughts, they automatically start to change.

You actually start to have fewer thoughts. And the thoughts you do have begin to shift towards being more helpful.

Basically, when your thoughts are just running on auto-pilot, hidden from your awareness, they're constant and chaotic. They're the incessant loops of fear, worry, doubt…etc.

That's why when you first tune into your thoughts, you think you're crazy. Because you're bringing awareness to that looping chaos for the first time. But if you continue to bring awareness consistently, the thoughts dissipate and harmonize.

When you bring awareness to your thoughts, you also give yourself the power of choice.

You can choose to think thoughts that are helpful. And that's so powerful.

Imagine if you were able to hand-pick every thought you ever had... Do you think it would make your life better? Of course.

You can get closer to that "ideal" of hand-picking every thought by practicing observing your thoughts consistently.

Become A Master of Thought

Most people are a slave to their thoughts.

If their monkey mind slips into a loop of worry, they're just along for the ride. It sucks most people in before they realize it. This keeps us trapped in unhelpful patterns.

And the crazy thing is that it's so hard to catch. These incessant thoughts only go on because they're unconscious. You don't realize it, well, until you realize it. Ha!

But once you bring awareness to your thoughts, you're back in your position of power.

If you're reading this, here's your invitation to reclaim your throne and be the master of thoughts, instead of a slave to them.

It's just two simple things…
1. **Observe your thoughts as often as possible**
2. **Choose better thoughts whenever you observe unhelpful thoughts**

Do this right now. Pause, take three deep breaths and bring your awareness to your thoughts. What's going on in your head? Just watch it.

If it's helpful, smile and enjoy. If it's not helpful, choose a more helpful thought.

It's really that simple, but it does require consistent practice.

If you can do this even once per day, it will change your life in a major way over the next few months and years. It literally takes 10 seconds, so there's really no excuses.

This is how we reprogram our mind. And since everything we see around us begins as a thought, imagine what your life will look like if you only think helpful thoughts.

Chapter 3: Emotions

Main Question:
What Emotions Am I Feeling Right Now?

Just like thoughts, emotions are so familiar, yet hard to describe.

Everyone feels emotions. But what are they? You can't see them, but you experience them. And you definitely see their effects. I mean, have you ever seen someone really angry?

Emotions are states of being. That's the simplest way of describing them.

Another way of viewing emotions is as archetypal energies. Energies in motion. They're like templates of energy that we experience, ranging from despair, to anger, to contentment, to pure bliss.

Now here's the relationship between thoughts and emotions.

When a certain amount of related thoughts occur, they build together to the point of being felt. These are emotions.

If you think about things that make you angry, you'll soon feel angry. If you think about things that are joyful, you'll soon feel joyful.

Tracing Back to Awareness

Because emotions are undeniably felt, they're a great way of "knowing" the thoughts that are going on in your head.

If you can feel that you're angry, you naturally become aware that you're thinking angry thoughts. And with that awareness, those thoughts are no longer going on auto-pilot. You have the choice to change those angry thoughts, or let go of them completely.

By bringing "feeling awareness" to emotions, you uncover the underlying thoughts that created the state that you're in.

Learn to feel. When you feel, your thoughts are revealed to your awareness.

But if you're constantly thinking, you're locked in the world of thought. And when you're locked in the world of thought, how can you have a bird's eye view of your thoughts? You can't. This is how thinking becomes a loop, and most of the time, we're not even aware of it.

It's like the old expression, the fish are the last to be aware of the water. Why? Because it's their whole world. If thinking is your entire world, you're lost in thought without knowing any different.

When you learn to feel, you transcend the world of thinking and look at it from a bird's eye view. This puts you in a position of power and self-mastery.

Emotions Are Currents

Emotions are closely associated with the element of water.

They flow, they wash over you, and they can even drown you. Also, in symbolism and dream interpretation, emotions are represented by water.

So how can we actually leverage this connection of emotions and water? Let them flow.

Emotions need to flow.

What happens if anger is dammed up over years and years? It eventually gets to a breaking point, where you have an explosion of anger.

A lot of people suppress emotions, and they eventually lead to some kind of breaking point, whether it be an explosion or some kind of dis-ease.

That's one extreme. The other extreme is the person who takes their emotions out on everyone. Sure, the emotions are moving, but if your life is a constant tsunami, nothing has the chance to grow.

Anger is the easiest example to understand, so let's go back to that.

You don't want to suppress anger, because that will lead to an explosion, or some kind of ailment. You also don't want to indiscriminately take anger out on everyone. Not only is that harmful to the people around you, you make your own life a non-stop storm of anger (which obviously isn't enjoyable).

So, what's the balance?

The balance of emotions comes from two things:
1. **Awareness** - Being aware of the emotions you're feeling
2. **Healthy expression** - Expressing emotions in a healthy way

Awareness is becoming a common theme here. If you're unaware of your emotions, you're a slave to them. This is what leads to unconsciously causing chaos to yourself and others.

There's a reason why we use the expression, "possessed by anger." Because it's unconscious. No one really wants to be angry. It's no fun. But they can't help it. There are unconscious patterns going on. And until awareness is brought to it, it perpetuates on auto-pilot.

The second step is healthy expression. This means expressing emotions in a way that doesn't cause harm to yourself or others. You need awareness to do this though, because **expressing emotions in a healthy way is a conscious choice.**

If you're feeling angry, first of all, bring it to full awareness. Feel the anger and watch it, instead of getting possessed by it and reacting. When you bring awareness to the anger, you have a choice. You can go outside and scream. You can lock yourself in your car and scream. You can go for a run. You can take some deep breaths.

There are many tools for expressing emotions in a healthy way. The more awareness you have, and the more tools at your disposal, the more you become a master of your emotions.

Tools of Expression

Here's a list of tools for expressing emotions in a healthy way:

Anger:

- Scream in your car
- Scream outside
- Punch a punching bag
- Go for a run
- Workout
- Do some breathwork

Sadness:
- Cry
- Cry in your car
- Cry into a pillow
- Write a letter or journal

Resentment:
- Ho'oponopono*
- Write a letter or journal
- Affirm forgiveness out loud

Ho'oponopono is an ancient Hawaiian Huna method for forgiveness. It's just visualizing the person or situation you wish to forgive and repeating to yourself, "I love you. I'm sorry. Please forgive me. Thank you."

Those are just some ideas. But there's no limit here. And a lot of those can be applied to different emotions too. Like if you're feeling envious of someone, maybe journaling about it would help.

We even suppress positive emotions too. Remember to express your positive emotions. There's discretion with this too. You don't want to break out into song and dance when someone is giving a presentation. Or maybe you do…

Emotional mastery comes with consistent practice. You'll find that the more you practice awareness and healthy expression, the less of a grip emotions have on you. You'll be able to watch the unhelpful emotions pass, and "surf" the more positive emotions.

Emotionless is a Lie

People who say they're emotionless are really just numb to emotions.

The emotions still come and go, but they've built such a pattern of suppression that they're not even felt.

We see this in so many people. People who pack on massive amounts of muscle because they're angry and scared. People who emotionally eat because it calms them down. People who drink alcohol to numb the underlying hum of sadness they feel.

I've done it myself, with all of those examples. I remember telling people that "I never get angry." But I later realized that I was just really good at suppressing anger. I got angry a lot, but I built a habit of "swallowing" it. This resulted in me being obsessed with working out, using my unresolved anger to fuel my workouts. It wasn't until I admitted that I feel angry sometimes that it felt like a dark cloud over me went away.

Most of us are masters of suppression, especially men. Early on in life, we're taught that anger is bad (even if expressed in a healthy way). We're taught that crying is a weakness. We're even taught that expressing too much joy is weird. What does this lead to? A habit of suppressing emotions.

Would you want to live life completely numb to emotions?

What we're all looking for in life is some kind of feeling. Most goals we set, even the things we want, are really the desire for some kind of feeling.

We want that nice house because it will make us feel safe, secure and at peace. We want an amazing relationship because it will bring love, acceptance and joy. People want to be able to quit their job and travel the world because it will feel like freedom.

Everything we want in life comes down to some kind of feeling. And it's usually emotions like joy, peace, bliss, love, freedom, serenity, happiness...etc.

But there's a catch.... These feelings are only genuine and sustaining when they're generated from within. When your joy, for example, is generated from within, it's not dependent on circumstance. You don't "need" something to feel joy. You choose to feel joyful as you move through life, not only when you achieve or get something.

This simple shift makes you your own perpetual energy generator. And here's the cool thing. This whole book helps you become this way, as a natural extension of who you are.

Emotions, Current & Energy

Emotions are raw energy. They provide you with current.

If you think about it, current is a word used for both water and energy. There's no coincidence there. That's because emotions have a lot to do with your energy levels.

Here are some examples...
- Ever notice an increase in strength when you feel motivated?
- Ever notice a surge of energy when you get angry, then feel drained afterwards?
- Ever feel as energetic as a child when you experience joy?
- Ever feel a calm sense of empowerment when you're at peace?

Emotions are current. Learn to use the current to your advantage. When you master emotions, you master your current.

With awareness, you have the choice. You can let the unhelpful emotions pass, or express them in a healthy way. And you can ride the waves of helpful emotions.

Tune in. You are the master of your reality.

Chapter 4: The "Real" You

Main Question:
What is Driving Me?

Let's spiral back to the question, "Who am I?"

The most accurate answer, using words is simply, "I am."

I know. For some people this seems so intangible or vague. But if you let go of trying to over-analyze it, it's really simple and practical.

"I am" just means pure awareness. In many traditions, this is called "the observer."

Let's continue to make this experiential.

Close your eyes, take three deep breaths, and ask yourself these questions again…
- "Who is the thinker of my thoughts?"
- "Who is the observer of the thinker of my thoughts?"

Don't "try" to answer the questions. Just let the questions themselves integrate into your being. Simply observe. Give yourself a few moments to let each question integrate.

Go ahead and do that right now, before continuing reading.

∞

Remember, this is a practice.

The more often you do this, the more you acquaint with this essence of who we all are.

It's like any relationship. If you just see someone in the distance occasionally, you don't really have a relationship.

This is how most people are with their inner observer. They might catch glimpses of it during a few moments of their life, but that's about it.

I'm not saying it's easy. We live in a world that labels us in hundreds of different ways. And we take on those labels, stories and programs as our identity. On top of that, we're constantly distracted.

We've been conditioned to be fixated on the external world, at the expense of our body, mind and emotional well-being. And completely covering the observer underneath it all.

What's Driving Me?

Another question that sparks massive awareness is, "What's driving me?"

With anything you're doing, ask yourself that question, and be completely honest with yourself.

When you're reaching for that 10th cookie, ask yourself, "What's driving me?" It's probably some combination of addiction, pleasure or habit.

When you're thinking obsessively over how someone wronged you, ask yourself, "What's driving me?" Chances are, it's resentment, spite, anger, hatred…etc.

For those peak moments of bliss in life, what do you think was driving you?

Now we're getting somewhere.

"What's driving me?" is another deep question. Because it naturally leads to other questions like, "Who is 'me'? And if something else is driving me, then who am I and what's going on?"

Yet even asking this question creates awareness. And what is our truest self? Pure awareness. So the question, "What is driving me?" allows you to tune into pure awareness (your real self) and transcend programmed behaviors.

That simple question has the power to shatter illusions and return you to that pure awareness that opens you up to all possibility.

Awareness is Practical

I used to think meditation and all of that "inner" stuff was escapism. I thought people were doing it to avoid the world.

But here's the kicker… Learning how to observe with pure awareness is actually the most practical thing you can do.

Think about it…

CEO's need to be able to take a step back and observe their company from a neutral point of view in order to ensure the company thrives.

Any athlete needs to be in a state of pure awareness to perform at a high level. If they get lost in over-analysis, they slip up.

Awareness of all kinds of cultural and political influences (especially the subtle kinds that most don't see) is what makes a great journalist.

Awareness is THE prerequisite for any new action in your life. If you want to create a new habit, you need awareness. If you want to start a new career, you need awareness. You need awareness to forge any new path for yourself.

I've had so many hiking experiences where I get lost in thought. And what happens? In my auto-pilot of thinking, instead of being aware of my surroundings, I've gotten lost a few times.

But when I'm in pure awareness, just observing everything, without even thinking, I know exactly where I am and where I need to go.

In life, most people are on auto-pilot, lost in thought. And what happens? They mindlessly wander, getting more lost in the process. Yet with awareness, you navigate with clarity, reaching the peaks in life, and seamlessly find your way back home.

This leads us to one of the superpowers that comes out of awareness: CHOICE. With awareness, you put yourself in a position to make conscious choices, instead of reacting or continuing patterns unconsciously.

Chapter 5: The Power of Choice

Main Question:
Do I Have a Choice Right Now?

The main question for this chapter is, "Do I have a choice right now?"

It's a trick question, because even saying "no" is a choice. So the answer is always "yes." You do have a choice, in every moment.

If you feel like you don't, the rest of this chapter will reveal a lot for you.

<u>Choice is a superpower.</u>

We hinted at this earlier. But it deserves its own chapter.

Choice and power are so related that they're almost synonymous.

Here's what I mean. More choices equal a wider range of possibilities for your life. And the ability to consciously choose allows you to consciously create your life.

In the book The Structure of Magic (a foundational book in the world of therapy), Richard Bandler and John Grinder describe our power of choice like this...

> *"People end up in pain, not because the world is not rich enough to allow them to satisfy their needs, but because their representation of the world is impoverished. Correspondingly, then, the strategy that we as therapists adopt is to connect the client with the world in some way which gives them a richer set of choices."*

Think about it. People fall into a victim mentality because they don't believe they have a choice. People create unhelpful lifestyles through patterned behaviors operating on auto-pilot.

Let's paint a picture here... What would your life look like if you consciously chose every thought and action?

Obviously, all of your thoughts would be directed towards what you want in life. And so would every action.

If you really wanted to live in Hawaii, and you directed every thought and action towards that, it's inevitably going to happen. But most people will say they want to live in Hawaii, then proceed to list reasons why they can't. So that initial thought gets drowned out by thousands of excuses and limitations. And what happens? They continue their life of unconscious patterns. No Hawaii.

I'm not downplaying unfortunate circumstances in life. There are people in horrible situations all over the world. That's reality.

The purpose of this message is to show that there's always a choice, no matter how bleak life may seem.

Viktor Frankl, a holocaust survivor, sums it up beautifully in two quotes…

"Forces beyond your control can take away everything you possess except one thing, your freedom to choose how you will respond to the situation."

"Between stimulus and response there is a space. In that space is our power to choose our response. In our response lies our growth and our freedom."

If you're reading this, you're probably not in a concentration camp like Viktor Frankl was. So that means you have even more range of physical choices right now.

Start with realizing that you always can choose your response, no matter the circumstance. When you can consciously choose a response (or even to not respond at all), no matter what situation you're in, you are free.

Here's a simple example. If someone yells at you, the typical default reaction would be to yell back.

But if you bring awareness to that stimulus (someone yelling at you), you create the space to choose. Then you have the power to choose your response. You can choose to yell back, shrug it off, walk away, or even say something nice to them.

You're no longer a bundle of predictable reactions. You're free.

Does anyone really want to be a slave to unconscious reactions? Of course not. But they keep governing our lives until we cultivate awareness.

Your recognition of your choice, in every situation, is freedom.

> *"Living in bondage I have set myself free:*
> *I have broken away from the clutch of all narrowness."*
> ~ Kabir

That quote addresses that heart of freedom.

When you're aware of your power of choice, regardless of external circumstances, you've achieved ultimate freedom.

Most people have conditioned themselves to be dependent on external circumstances for their freedom. If you think something needs to be a certain way to be free, you've given away your freedom.

If you think you need to be rich to be free, you've already enslaved yourself. If you think you need a big house to be free, you've already enslaved yourself. If you think you need to be on a beach to be free, you've already enslaved yourself.

Freedom is your unconditional recognition of your power of choice, always.

Take a moment to acknowledge your inner freedom, right now…

> *I am aware of my power of choice, right now.*
> *I choose to choose.*
> *I am free.*

From here, you open up new worlds of possibility. From this space of freedom, you can choose your responses, your thoughts and your actions. This is how you create the life you want.

You must be diligent. You must continuously bring awareness to your thoughts, weeding out the unhelpful patterns and replanting helpful ones.

When you exercise your power of choice consistently, your power of choice grows. The more it grows, the wider your range of possibility.

Remember, in every moment, you have the power of choice.

What are you choosing?

Chapter 6: Big Ship, Small Rudder

Main Question:
What is One Little Shift I Can Make Today?

"Look at the ships also: though they are so large and are driven by strong winds, they are guided by a very small rudder wherever the will of the pilot directs."
~ James 3:4

That quote is a beautiful analogy.

Your real self, pure awareness, is the pilot. From a state of awareness, you have the power of choice. Exercising your power of choice is the pilot guiding the ship with a small rudder.

The big ship of your life actually has a small rudder. That rudder is your power of choice. Even the smallest choices. And slight shifts in the rudder produces big changes in direction, especially over long periods of time.

The little things add up. Small, simple things produce huge results.

Creating big changes in your life is surprisingly simple. It consists of two things.
1. **Small Shifts**
2. **Consistency**

Change is simple, but definitely not easy. And the less aware you are, the harder it is.

It all comes back to awareness. From this space of awareness, you can choose to make small shifts in your life.

Again, imagine your life is like a boat. All it takes is a slight change in direction to create a big difference in where you go over the long-term. You just need to consistently move in that slightly different direction.

Make small shifts when you feel you need to change direction. They can come in many forms: mindset shifts, shifts in what you do, shifts in how you approach things, shifts in your focus…etc.

Here are some examples of small shifts that produce big results over time…

Realizing that it's actually possible to do something: Maybe it's getting healthy and fit, starting a business, finding an amazing relationship or living in your dream home. There's always that moment when something clicks, and you say to yourself, "Wow, I can actually do this."

It's the simple little mindset shifts, or a new way of approaching something in your life, that create exponential results over time.

Here are some more examples.

Learning something that saves you a lot of time and energy: This could be anything from a daily productivity hack to realizing just how much time and energy you waste people pleasing, or scrolling through social media.

Learning to organize your ideas to increase your creativity and productivity: This could be as simple as writing a to-do list every day to organize your thoughts.

Listening to audiobooks instead of the radio to learn more: Instead of listening to the radio, it's a simple shift to listen to audiobooks instead. This way, you can learn and develop skills without extra time or effort.

Viewing your parents as little kids when you have problems with them: Seeing everyone you interact with as little kids, especially your parents, puts things into perspective. Adults are just little kids who grew. So when someone gets angry, seeing them as a child throwing a temper tantrum will actually help you not react to them. And you'll also see that everyone is just a little child looking for love and acceptance.

When you see an angry person, having the mentality that you don't know what they're going through: Maybe they're having the worst day of their life. You don't know. Again, everyone's just a little kid inside.

Instead of complaining, finding something positive to say: This simple shift completely changes your day, and your life, for the better.

Writing one thing you're grateful for every day can shift your mood for a whole day: This is another thing that completely upgrades your day and your life.

Not watching tv or looking at your phone while eating: This simple shift helps you be more present, and truly enjoy food.

Those are some examples of small, simple shifts.

After creating small shifts, the next step is to consistently move towards your vision.

Chapter 7: Small Daily Steps

Main Question:
What is One Small Step I Can Take Every Day to Move in a Positive Direction?

With anything you wish to achieve, small daily steps are what bring you there.

A lot of people have no vision, leaving them "lost at sea" and a victim of circumstance.

Most people, however, have at least a general idea of what they want. But it's vague. And they get overwhelmed by how big it is, so they don't even know where to start.

The key is to take small daily steps.

How do you hike a mountain? One step at a time. How do you eat an elephant? One bite at a time.

While I don't encourage elephant eating, I do encourage small daily steps.

Most people think writing a book is overwhelming, but not with small daily steps. If you want to write a book, commit to writing 2 pages per day. After just 100 days, you have a 200-page book. Anyone can write 2 pages a day. So with consistency, anyone can write a book.

Same thing with working out. Yeah, it's overwhelming to lose a lot of fat or pack on muscle. But if you focus on exercising for even 20 minutes per day, you're going to have a new body after a few months.

If you want to drop a bad habit or addiction, it's the same process. Focus on winning today. That's it. Never relapsing for the rest of your life is overwhelming. Just getting through today is easy. Then you focus on the next day, and the next, and it builds life-changing momentum.

If you want to start a business, that can be overwhelming too. But if you focus on taking one step every day towards building your business, you're going to make an incredible amount of progress over a year.

If you want to move into a nicer home (but can't afford it yet), think about the first step you can take. Maybe the first step is cutting some expenses you don't need. You do this every day until all unnecessary expenses are gone. Then you might focus on getting a raise, or getting a better job. You focus on this every day until you're making more money in some way. Then you can start looking at homes. These are all small steps that, when combined, have you living in a nicer home.

See the theme here? A lot of the big visions we have in life can be really overwhelming, especially when you just look at the whole thing. That's why most people never start. Or they start with a lot of motivation, then give up after a week or two.

But if you break any big vision down to small daily steps, it's actually a lot simpler than you think.

The book example perfectly explains this:
- Writing a book = Really overwhelming
- Writing 2 pages per day = Doable for anyone

Focus on Systems, Not Goals

Small daily steps are a system. It's a process that you apply daily.

Like we just looked at, big goals can be overwhelming. And what's a goal without a process to get there? It's just a quixotic dream.

So here's the recipe:
1. **Know the direction you wish to move in**
2. **Take small daily steps**

This way, the process automatically achieves the goal. Not only that, you begin to enjoy the process. This is what creates fulfillment.

When I made working out a routine for myself, I started to love it after a few weeks. When I started writing every day, I was loving it after a few weeks. This isn't just me. It happens to anyone who takes small daily steps towards something they genuinely want.

When you learn to love the journey as much as the destination, you live in continuous fulfillment. But if you're always chasing the next goal, you're never fulfilled.

Simple daily steps help you achieve goals more effectively AND make the process more enjoyable. How's that for a win-win?

Each Step Creates More Clarity

When you take small daily steps, your vision becomes clearer with every step you take.

With each step, you see a little more of the path. You see the next phase that you haven't seen before. Or you see it in more detail.

> *The car needs to be in motion for the steering to work.*

As you move, you can make slight adjustments to your direction. In fact, you WILL make slight adjustments to your direction.

There are people who cling inflexibly to goals, which can be a trap. Maybe the goal you had was something you thought you wanted, but you don't want now. That's ok. Allow yourself to make changes in your direction.

When I was 21, I had a radically different vision for myself than when I was 26. So if I rigidly held onto a long-term goal I set as my 21-year-old self, I would've created a life where I wasn't truly fulfilled.

Let your path adapt and evolve as you do. But still move in the direction you feel in your heart. There's a balance you must find, between persistence and the openness to change direction sometimes. That balance is unique to all of us, and it's learned through experience.

This chapter can be summed up in three steps:
1. **Know the direction you wish to move in**
2. **Take small daily steps**
3. **Find your balance with persistence and adaptation**

There's a warning here though. Most people "think" they know the direction they want to move in. They "think" they know their vision. But oftentimes, it's them chasing someone else's dream.

That's what the next chapter is about. We're going to get clear on that vision, and make sure it's 100% genuine. Because so many times, we get led astray without even realizing it.

Chapter 8: Why Are You Here?

Main Question:
Why Am I Here?

To get clear on your true vision, you need to ask yourself the "BIG" questions…

The ones that make you uncomfortable. The ones that scare you. The ones that you reflexively dismiss because you already think you know everything.

I first started asking myself some big, meaningful questions after almost killing myself…

- *Who am I?*
- *Is there more than just this physical reality?*
- *What's my purpose?*
- *Why am I here on Earth?*
- *How can I stop these bad habits?*
- *How can I be happy?*
- *What can I do to grow as a person?*

All of these questions, and more, became a daily search for me, after one fateful night.

I was in college. And I was at the lowest point of my life. I fought with my parents almost every time I talked to them, I neglected my sister and brother, my grades were terrible, I was desperately trying to fit in and be viewed as "cool" among my peers, my self-confidence was non-existent, I had overwhelming social anxiety and I drank until I blacked out 2-3 times per week.

One night I went to a party at a friend's house. Like most nights, I was drowning my sorrows in alcohol. I was damn good at it too. I would chug beers, take shots, whatever it took to escape. And though I considered it fun, there was so much pain beneath the empty, drunken smile.

After getting really drunk, we ended up going to another person's house, who happened to have a massive liquor collection. The last thing I remember was taking a few shots…

I woke up in the hospital.

Apparently, someone found me in a parking lot at 5am, passed out on the hood of a car. And when they measured my blood alcohol content at the hospital, it was 0.31 (0.4 is death). That was hours after I stopped drinking! So let's just say that I have guardian angels. I'm lucky to be alive.

I called my mom later that day, after I was released from the hospital. She wasn't mad at me, she was just really, really sad. I was filled with fear, guilt and anxiety. I remember lying in bed that night, thinking that my heart was stopping. But it kept on beating. And I was grateful to be alive.

Over the next few days, I had some more conversations with my mom and a trip to the school psychologist. Once the fear, guilt and anxiety dissipated, I started soul searching.

There was something within me, an inner calling, that I knew I had to follow.

That's when I started to ask myself some big, meaningful questions…
- *Who am I?*
- *Am I really ready to die right now?*

- *Is there more than just this physical reality?*
- *What's my purpose?*
- *Why am I here on Earth?*
- *How can I stop these bad habits?*
- *How can I be happy?*
- *What can I do to grow as a person?*

Even just entertaining questions like these sent a wave of energy through my body. I'd never experienced anything like it, so I kept following that calling.

It led me to discover self-help books. It led me to journaling. It led me to eating healthy It led me to develop a love for fitness. It led me to love nature. It led me to meditation.

Since that "rock bottom" moment, I've gradually been grounding myself deeper and deeper into love. It's been quite the journey. And it continues to this day.

Maybe you're in a rock bottom moment right now. Maybe you're not. Maybe you're at a high point. Either way, the "big" questions will bring you so much clarity.

The "Big" Questions

Make a habit out of asking yourself the big questions in life.

That's why we started this book off with the most fundamental question, "Who am I?"

Questions are so powerful. They're the basis of learning and growth. Questions are open doors to new worlds you've never explored.

When it comes to the big, deep questions, I've narrowed down a few that produce a lot of clarity around your purpose and big vision for your life.

I recommend going through the questions, picking one that resonates with you, and journaling about it.

Don't try to force answers. Let your realizations flow as the questions integrate into your being.
As you integrate these questions, and other big questions, your vision for your life will become clearer and clearer.

Here they are...
- What excites me?
- What kind of ideas come to me in the shower?
- What kind of things do people always ask me about?
- What topics do I regularly read about?
- During which experiences in my life have I felt the most alive?
- What unique interests, or abilities, did I have as a young child?
- What would I be doing if money were no object?
- What would I be doing if I absolutely, 100%, did not care about what other people think?
- What is on my bucket list?
- What topics can I blend together to create my own unique niche?
- If I were to write a short (1-2 sentence) "About Me", describing the ideal version of myself, what would it be?
- What causes do I strongly believe in, or connect with?
- What activities make me lose track of time?
- If I had to teach something, what would I teach?

- What challenges or obstacles have I overcome in life?

After reading through that list, you probably have some ideas coming through.

Again, I recommend picking one and journaling your response to it. Just let the words flow, without judgment.

With these questions, you don't need a definitive answer. You just need a feeling as to the direction you're moving in.

These questions are so powerful that it can be hard to put your answers into words. So contemplate them and let them integrate. As you do this, your direction becomes clearer and clearer.

Flowing Focus

When it comes to the question, "Why am I here?" there is a balance we all must find.

This unique balance is between floundering non-commitment and stubborn, rigid commitment.

Those are the two extremes. Floundering, non-commitment leaves you overwhelmed and running in circles, with no progress. Rigid commitment has you forcing everything and exhausting yourself, even when it's clearly time to change direction a bit.

It's crucial to have a direction. That's your purpose. But don't get so attached to it that it can't ever change. Allow your journey to be flowing focus.

This leads us into a technique that strengthens this flowing focus...

"Is This Mine?"

Most of your desires aren't your own...

Most of your goals aren't your own...

What I mean by this is simple. We've all picked up all kinds of programming throughout our lives. It comes from everywhere; parents, family, school, media, pop culture, hollywood...etc.

Since birth, other people have been telling us what we need to do, what's good for us, what a good life looks like, and all that stuff.

We've been swimming in an ocean of other people's programs our whole lives. The result? Most people have no idea about what they truly want in life.

We THINK we know what we want, but most often, when you really look into it, you realize it's a program you picked up… Not what YOU truly want from the depths of your soul.

That's why it's so important, with every desire or goal you have, to ask the question, "Is this mine?"

With every idea, vision, goal or desire you have…. With everything that throws you off emotionally… Pause and ask yourself, "Is this mine?"

9 times out of 10, it's not. It's a program you've taken on from somewhere (parents, school, media, society in general…etc.). Stop wasting energy on programs you've taken on and allow the clarity of your soul to shine through.

How Do You Know?

The difference between your true vision and other people's programs can be hard to detect.

There's always hints though. Here are some ways you can discern for yourself...

Symptoms of someone else's programs:
- Feeling forced
- Not fun
- Having to chase everything
- Unfulfilling
- Something you think you "have" to do
- Someone loses and someone else wins (win-lose scenarios)

Indicators of something being true to your soul:
- It feels expansive
- It feels flowing
- You feel your creativity unleashed
- Your imagination expands
- You start to become magnetic and attract people
- You feel joyful when you think about doing it
- A win-win for yourself and other people

Here's a fun way to cut through the programs...

The Alien Thought Experiment

Imagine yourself as an alien who just teleported into your body right now.

You have no attachment to human culture or history. You look around and see the world from a neutral perspective. Your mental and emotional awareness is at the peak of what you can imagine.

What would you do with the rest of your life? What would you work towards? What kind of impact would you make? How would you go about your day?

This simple thought experiment can reveal a lot.

Chapter 9: Infinite Possibility

Main Question:
What Conditions Am I Placing on My life?

Everything we've discussed so far leads to this…

Infinite Possibility.

When you believe, wholeheartedly, that anything is possible, guess what happens? Opportunities come to you that you never would have imagined. Amazing things just happen, that you couldn't plan or predict. Doors open that you didn't even know existed.

Successful people in any area of life (business, relationships, happiness, spiritual growth, sports…etc.) always stay open to infinite possibility.

Why would you ever want to put limitations on what's possible?

That sounds insane, right? But most people do it every day.

Why? Because they want to play it safe. It's so insidious that even suffering can become safe, because it's a familiar habit.

We see this with people who struggle with addictions. In their heart, they know they're creating suffering, but they continue because it's a familiar pattern. We see this with obesity. They know they're destroying their health, yet they continue their unhealthy ways because it's familiar. There's an odd, yet irresistible comfort in familiar habits, even when they're destructive.

If you're courageous enough to venture outside of your mental walls, magic happens.

Who's to say that the opportunity you've been waiting for your whole life won't appear today? And if it did, are you willing to accept it? Or are you too comfortable?

It's time to get really honest with yourself.

Think about the one thing you want most in life. Now ask yourself these questions…
- Do I believe I deserve it?
- Would I be willing to accept it if it came into my life today?

If you answered no to either of those, you're lying to yourself.

Everyone deserves to live an amazing, fulfilling life. If you think otherwise, you're only limiting yourself and creating unnecessary suffering. Even you reading this is helping you let go of that.

If you're not willing to accept your biggest dream into your life right now, check yourself. Do you not feel worthy? Does the change intimidate you? Why do you want to limit yourself? Why do you want to play it safe?

Here's what you get to embody…
- If your dream job presents itself, you have the courage to apply for it
- If you see your dream romantic partner on the street, you have the courage to introduce yourself

- If someone offers to help you with something, gratefully accepting the help
- If you really want to help someone, helping them without hesitation
- If any opportunity to better yourself comes up, you do it

Why wouldn't you do these things? If we look at limitations with complete objectivity, it's as simple as this... You've created conditions for yourself, and it's not helpful at all.

Conditions

Here's where we directly confront the main question of this chapter... What conditions am I placing on my life?

These words get tossed around all the time... "Conditioning", "Programming", "Limiting Beliefs."

They can seem like really woo-woo things that are hard to conceptualize, let alone change.

But I've realized that "conditions" are actually simple to innerstand. They're simply a mode of operating.

People use conditions with computer programming to get certain results.

Conditions inherently limit data to only see a specific set of it. While this can be useful for analyzing sets of data, it becomes severely limiting when our whole lives are based around rigid conditions. Here are some common ones...

- If someone acts like that, then I get angry.
- If I can't watch my favorite show, I can't enjoy myself.
- If I don't drink, then I can't have fun at social gatherings
- I need to work in finance to make good money
- I need my coffee in the morning to function
- I need to be rich in order to travel
- I need to screw people over to be rich
- I can't be as fit as those other people
- If I have to wait in line, I get impatient
- I'll be happy when I'm retired
- I'll be happy when I find that special someone

Those are all conditions! See the themes here?
- If this, then that
- I need X to be happy

- I can't do X because X

This is exactly like a computer program!

And here's the real kicker... 99% of the conditions that we create just aren't true. Let's look at the examples again:
- If someone acts like that, then I get angry → You can choose not to react
- If I can't watch my favorite show, I can't enjoy myself → There's a million other ways to enjoy yourself.
- If I don't drink, then I can't have fun at social gatherings → You can choose to have fun in any situation, with or without any substance.
- I need to work in finance to make good money → There are millions of ways to make "good" money.
- I need my coffee in the morning to function → You can function without coffee. There's lots of people functioning perfectly fine without coffee.
- I need to be rich in order to travel → You don't have to spend millions to travel.

- I need to screw people over to be rich → You can get rich by selling products or services that help people.
- I can't be as fit as those other people → You can be as fit as you want.
- If I have to wait in line, I get impatient → You can choose to be patient.
- I'll be happy when I'm retired → Why not be happy now? Why wait?
- I'll be happy when I find that special someone → Again, why not be happy now? Why wait?

Do you see how we limit ourselves with all of these conditions? Most people are walking around with thousands of these conditions in their head. No wonder why so many people feel limited, stuck and like a victim. Their minds are filled with conditions.

Now I'm not saying to throw away all conditions. That's not even possible, because that's how our minds operate. What I'm saying is to consciously choose each condition you have.

Create conditions that are helpful, and let go of the ones that aren't. This allows you to be open to the amazing possibilities that are all around you, at all times. But with limiting conditions, you can't see them. And even if you could, you would dismiss it because it's outside of your range of possibility. This is how most people can be their own worst enemy.

What people call "positive affirmations" are actually helpful, empowering conditions.

The goal with affirmations is to replace your unhelpful conditions with conditions that actually help you. It's rewriting your mind-body computer codes.

When used correctly, positive affirmations will change your programs and your life. But you have to do it the right way. For affirmations to really work, you need to reprogram your subconscious mind. Don't worry, we'll get deep into subconscious reprogramming soon.

The Stories We Tell

We all tell ourselves stories, based on the conditions we're running in our minds.

We tell our own biased versions of what happened in the past. We bring those biases into the present moment, coloring our experience with it. And we project those biased stories into the future, limiting our opportunities moving forward.

When you're telling yourself limiting stories, you create the same types of things over and over again in your life. Like Admiral Ackbar in Star Wars said, "It's a trap!"

So here are a few questions for you...
- How would you describe the events leading up to your life now?
- What situations or events are you choosing to emphasize?
- Are you the hero of your story, or the victim? (Remember, every hero goes through hardship)
- With the struggles in your life, are you focusing on being a victim or the lessons you learned?

I invite you to write all of those questions down and journal about them. It will reveal a lot about the stories you're telling yourself.

There are an infinite number of sides to every story, and there are an infinite number of ways to interpret every situation.

In recent years, it's been revealed that eyewitnesses aren't as reliable as you may think. Many false accusations regarding crimes are based on inaccurate eyewitness testimonies. And it's not because they're consciously lying. It's because there are so many factors that distort our perceptions and memory. These include poor lighting, distractions, stress, the effect of a police officer's body language during questioning, memories blending between the suspect lineup and the actual event...etc.

There are so many factors that distort our memories. And it's not only with traumatic incidents like crimes. This happens even with mundane events of daily life.

If 5 people experience the same thing, you're going to have 5 different stories. If you and 4 friends went out to dinner, there's going to be 5 different stories about that dinner. And that's a simple dinner! The more emotional an event is, and the further in the past it is, the more it gets distorted.

A fun experiment with this is to ask your parents and siblings about events in your childhood. You'll quickly realize how different everyone's version of the same events are.

Every time I've done this with my parents, my sister, or brother, their story has been different from mine. Sure, we agreed on general points (like, "Yeah that time we went to Disney World…"), but there's always differing perspectives about how it was and the details of what happened.

We all have unique perspectives, biases, different filters of how we view reality, and selective memory.

In our minds, we create our version of reality, and our persona of who we think we are. Then we try to make everything we experience fit into that picture. This is how our ego distorts reality. And if you don't bring awareness to these stories, it's easy to trap yourself in your own self-limiting world of delusion.

So, what kind of stories are you telling yourself? How are you interpreting the events of your life? Are you portraying yourself as a victim? Are you telling yourself you're always right and other people are wrong?

The Story of Your Best Self

Now let's shift the focus to the best version of yourself.

What qualities would the best version of yourself have?

Write down three of them right now. And specify exactly what you mean by these words too.

For example, I just wrote Focused, Noble and Creative.

By "focused" I mean having a clear vision and prioritizing what's important in life. By "noble" I mean embodying honesty, integrity, generosity, compassion, leadership and courage. By "creative" I mean expressing my uniqueness, exercising my imagination and living creatively.

Now tell your stories through the filter of those qualities.

With every story you're telling, whether it's to yourself or someone else, check that it's in alignment with the qualities of your best self. If it's not, either let that story go or tell it from the perspective of your best self.

For example, if I'm complaining about how bratty my step-daughter is, that's not noble. Instead of telling that story, I could talk about the progress she's made or just choose to focus on something else. It's not noble to complain. It's not noble to react with anger or judgment to other people's behavior. A noble person addresses situations directly, without being reactive. They remain grounded in their power amidst any storms of life.

Reframing how you tell stories (in your own head, or to other people) can shift a lot in your life.

So here are a few more simple questions:
- *How does your best self act?*
- *How does your best self speak?*
- *How does your best self treat other people?*
- *How does your best self treat yourself?*

I invite you to BE your best self for the rest of the day today. And keep evolving more and more into your best self from there.

The Power of Words

We code our reality, and create conditions, through words.

Both our inner and outer speech act as vehicles for our thoughts, and building blocks of our intention.

Words are spells. That's why we SPELL words.

We SENTENCE ourselves to TERMS. We use CURSE WORDS when we're angry. See how much is encoded in the language?

Many religious and spiritual texts hint at this:
- "Right Speech" is part of the Buddhist Eightfold Path
- In the book The Four Agreements by Don Miguel Ruiz, the first agreement is "Be Impeccable with Your Word"
- The famous biblical quote, "In the beginning was the word…"

Here are a few more biblical hints:
- *"By faith we understand that the universe was created by the word of God, so that what is seen was not made out of things that are visible." (Hebrews 11:3)*
- *"Death and life are in the power of the tongue, and those who love it will eat its fruits." (Proverbs 18:21)*

Of course, the power of words isn't limited to religious and spiritual contexts. The power of words is actually a commonsense, practical tool that we all have access to, at all times.

The poet Emily Dickinson said, *"I know nothing in the world that has as much power as a word. Sometimes I write one, and I look at it until it begins to shine."*

This isn't an exaggeration. It's literal.

If you think words aren't powerful, think about this…
- How do you get millions of people to go to war? Words.
- How do you get millions of people to follow a belief system? Words.
- How does every society even function? Words.

- How do you communicate with everyone in your life? Words.
- What's the difference between a child who feels empowered vs disempowered? Usually the words their parents spoke to them.

The pen truly is mightier than the sword. The pen, of course, refers to the power of words. One passionate speech can drive a whole world into war. Or if wielded differently, create world peace.

"Throughout human history, our greatest leaders and thinkers have used the power of words to transform our emotions, to enlist us in their causes, and to shape the course of destiny. Words can not only create emotions, they create actions. And from our actions flow the results of our lives."
~ Tony Robbins

As humans, words shape our world.

Our world is completely coated (or coded) with words.

Have you ever really thought about that? We even label everything we see and experience with words.

We see a tree and label it a tree. We experience an emotion and label it. We name each other.

We label everything all the time, to the point where, most of the time, we're not even aware of it. Our mind labels and defines everything in our experience.

How you define something determines the field you're playing on, and the game you're playing. Every time you define something, even subconsciously, you create a game with certain rules that you abide by.

If you define what a relationship is based on certain parameters, all of your actions in the relationship will be based on those parameters.

This is how, in relationships, you get situations where one person feels like their needs aren't met, and the other one is fine. They had two different definitions of a "good relationship" and never clearly communicated those definitions with each other (and often didn't even realize it themselves).

Most of the time, we automatically define everything, without knowing. This "boxes us in" with the definitions we create for ourselves and our lives.

Now here's where some more things are going to click for you…

Remember the truest answer to, "Who am I?"

I AM.

"I Am" is our truest self. It is our essence of pure awareness. It is the "God within."

So whenever you say, "I am…" you're literally calling upon the God within.

You are invoking your core self to help fulfill whatever comes after "I am."

If you say, "I am stupid," you're calling upon the most creative force in the universe to make yourself more stupid.

If you say, "I am worthy," you're calling upon the most creative force in the universe to make you worthier.

Every time you say, "I am", it's like picking up a seed (the creative force) and planting whatever it is you say after. The more of a specific kind of seed you plant, the more you'll see it in your life.

Saying "I'm worthy" a couple times probably won't change your life much. But what if you said it so often that it became your default self-talk? If your default self-talk was "I'm worthy," you would be repeating it thousands of times per day. With this, how could you not feel and act worthy in your life?

Remember, your words shape your emotions, which shape your actions. This is common sense.

When I was in high school and college, I used to be really nervous and anxious around girls. My self-talk was littered with anxious thoughts... *"Are they looking at me? What if I say something stupid? Do they think I'm cool?"* Guess what these thoughts created? Anxiety. Guess what the feeling of anxiety resulted in? Me being nervous and lacking confidence. Of course, everyone picked up on my nervousness, and I wasn't "successful" with girls. This created a self-fulfilling prophecy around my interactions with girls.

If someone had told me about the concepts in this book then, I would have realized that my self-talk was driving all of this. I would have brought awareness to my thoughts, and with that awareness, given myself the power to choose new thoughts. After a few days of doing this, my social anxiety would've dwindled in the light of self-confidence.

This goes way deeper than social anxiety too. Every day, bring awareness to the connection of your thoughts, your words, your emotions and your experience in the world.

Remember, your thoughts can keep you pinned down in the pit of despair, or raise you up into the life you've always dreamed of.

Take a moment to appreciate your access to this key. You now know about awareness, your power of choice, and how this can completely upgrade your life.

Breaking Out of Auto-Pilot

The more aware you become, the less you operate on auto-pilot.

You start to take a step back and look at default patterns. You see how so many of our thoughts, words and actions are programs running on auto-pilot (most of which are not helpful). And they will continue to run on auto-pilot, until you bring awareness to it and choose to take the wheel.

An easy way to start breaking out of auto-pilot programs is to question commonly used phrases.

When you or someone else says a cliché statement out of habit, take a closer look at it. What's underneath it? See the truth in it, the falsehood in it, and the context it's used in.

For example, "Money can't buy happiness."

Obviously, money can't buy happiness. I've never seen happiness sold in a store. Plus, true happiness comes from within. But money can create more possibilities in your life, making it easier for you to see that inner happiness. Notice the context with this platitude too. Is it being used to justify hatred, frustration or limiting beliefs around money?

Another one is, "It is what it is."

Of course it is what it is! Whatever is happening now is happening now. With this platitude, it's important to see what's behind it. Is it being used to justify complacency or victimhood? Or is it being used to fully accept the present moment, without resisting it, knowing that all situations are temporary? There's a big difference as to how it's used. And being aware of this context will allow you to see what's really underneath the things that yourself and other people say.

Do you robotically say "good" or "alright" when someone asks you how you're doing?

Do you constantly complain that whatever situation "sucks"? Do you gossip about people?

Bring awareness to everything you speak. It reveals a lot. This will, in turn, help you become more aware of your thoughts.

If you find yourself repeating a limiting platitude, consciously substitute it for something more helpful. Do this as many times as needed until you feel a shift. It might take weeks, or even months, but changing the way you speak and think inevitably changes you.

Re-member, words are spells. Your words shape your emotional state and inspire your actions. When you learn to consciously direct your words, you learn how to consciously direct your actions. And your life will only get better.

Chapter 10: Seeing Your New Life

Main Question:
What is an Affirming Belief I Choose to Reprogram My Mind With?

Just by reading this book, you're opening the door to a new life. And by applying the wisdom here, you step through that door into your new life.

In this chapter, we're getting into the reprogramming process. Yes indeedy. You're about to learn exactly how to reprogram your operating system (beliefs, conditions...etc.) in order to live your best life.

Subconscious Reprogramming

As humans, we have a conscious mind and a subconscious mind.

The conscious mind is the thinking and planning mind. The subconscious mind consists of our beliefs, emotions, habits, patterns, involuntary bodily functions, intuition, instincts, desires…etc.

The average person operates from their subconscious mind anywhere from 88%-95% of the time. This means the vast majority of everything we do is subconscious, meaning it's not a conscious choice.

If you really get honest with yourself, you'll notice that most of what you do is based in the subconscious mind; beliefs, habits, patterns, desires…etc.

Look at most people. They're pretty predictable. If you know someone, you can probably predict what they're going to do on an average Friday night. You can probably predict how they'll react to the latest political scandal. Right? That's because most people are coasting through life on an auto-pilot of subconscious programs.

We're uprooting that here.

The subconscious mind is like a recorder. Whatever you experience, whatever information you take in, gets automatically recorded into the subconscious mind. The subconscious mind records everything. This is why it's important to be aware of what you're taking in.

About 90% of your life is based on subconscious programs. Pretty interesting, right?

Now, how do you know what your subconscious programs are? Just look at your life.

Your life is a direct reflection of your subconscious programs.

What areas of your life do you have to try hard and force to get results? This means that your conscious mind is trying to overcome a subconscious program.

There are three main ways subconscious programs get established.

3 Methods of Subconscious Programming & Reprogramming
1. Hypnosis
2. Habituation
3. Peak Experiences

Hypnosis is a kind of trance state, characterized by heightened susceptibility to suggestion.

We've all seen or heard of stage hypnotists who somehow convince people they're eating an apple when it's really a potato. That's hypnosis for entertainment. But day-to-day hypnosis is much more subtle…

Deep hypnosis occurs when we're in a theta brainwave state. Children's brainwaves are in theta from about ages 2-6. Then from ages 6-12, our brainwaves are in alpha, which is light hypnosis.

This means that from ages 2-6, everything you experience, everything you're told, is downloaded straight into your subconscious mind via hypnosis. Everything is a hypnotic suggestion to a kid this age. This continues, though less and less, until about age 12.

These hypnotic brainwave states also occur when watching television, which puts the brain in a low alpha state (mild to moderate hypnosis, depending on the person). That's why it's called television PROGRAMMING. So be mindful of what you're watching, otherwise it's programming your mind in unhelpful, or even destructive, ways.

Other times the brain is in a hypnotic state are during deep relaxation and meditation, which are theta wave states (deep hypnosis). We also pass through theta when we're falling asleep, as well as waking up. Anything in your mind at these times is a direct hypnotic suggestion. We'll go more into this soon.

The second way to program the subconscious mind is through habituation, or repetition.

When we do things consistently, it gets ingrained in the subconscious mind.

This is how people are able to drive while they're daydreaming. Their subconscious mind is driving while their conscious mind is thinking about other stuff. Because people drive every day, it becomes a subconscious program.

The process of habituation applies to activities as well as beliefs. The more seeds you plant, through action, speech or self-talk, the more it becomes part of your subconscious mind.

The last way of programming the subconscious mind is through what I call *"peak experiences."*

Peak experiences are blips on your radar. They are moments that stand out from the rest, for better or worse.

Some peak experiences can be traumatic, while others can be extremely positive.

Traumatic experiences, like being in a war zone, can program the subconscious mind with fear. Because it's such an intense, peak experience, it goes straight into the subconscious mind as a prominent program.

The same thing happens with overwhelmingly positive experiences. These are experiences like traveling somewhere new, skydiving, watching the sunset over the ocean, being on top of a mountain and admiring the view with awe, someone giving you an amazing, heartfelt compliment, any kind of celebration...etc.

These positive peak experiences also affect your subconscious beliefs in a major way.

For example, if you live in Nebraska your whole life, and take a trip to India, you'll never be the same after. Being somewhere new, with a completely different culture and completely different landscapes, automatically reprograms your subconscious mind. It might expand your sense of possibility, make you more compassionate, make you less neurotic and controlling, make you more joyful, more peaceful, appreciate nature more, appreciate culture more...etc. It could be any of those, or more, according to who you are and what you experience.

How to Reprogram Your Subconscious Mind

Now that you know how the subconscious mind operates, let's talk about how to reprogram your subconscious mind.

With these tools, you will have the power to reprogram your subconscious mind to help you live your best life.

Let's go through the three ways to reprogram, with specific strategies for each.

Reprogramming Via Hypnosis

When it comes to hypnosis, you can't be in theta brainwave state all day like when you were 6. And most things on television aren't for your highest good (to say the least).

Note: There are hypnotherapists that reprogram your subconsciousness. But in this book, I aim to empower you to do it yourself.

So, if you want to reprogram your own subconscious mind via hypnosis, that brings us to deep relaxation, meditation and the time around sleep.

As noted before, our brains pass through theta state when we're falling asleep, as well as waking up. So anything in your mind at these times is a direct hypnotic suggestion. These are ideal times to reprogram your subconscious mind.

There are two ways to do this…

1) Subconscious Planting (DIY Version)

The first is what I call "subconscious planting." As you're falling asleep, plant a helpful idea in your subconscious mind. All you need to do is focus on a specific word and repeat it in your mind.

It can be something you want in your life or a quality you wish to embody. Just focus on it as you drift into sleep. When you do this, you're literally hypnotizing yourself for the better.

Do this as you're waking up too. As soon as you begin waking up, plant that thought, word or affirmation.

Here are some examples of words or phrases you can repeat to yourself while falling asleep or waking up:
- "Wealth"
- "I am wealthy"
- "I am worthy"
- "Bliss"
- "I am healthy"
- "Peace"
- "Courage"

Or you can get more specific if you want:
- "$10,000"

- "I am attracting my ideal partner"
- "I am living in my dream home"

Just get clear on what you want, and repeat something that feels good to you.

2) Subconscious Planting (Audio Recording)

The other way to reprogram your subconscious mind around sleep is to listen to positive audios as you sleep.

This could be an audiobook about a topic you want to embody more of, or positive affirmations.

Note: Be very mindful about what you choose to listen to. Because it's going straight to your subconscious mind, make sure it's of the highest integrity.

You can even record something yourself and play it while you sleep. Just record yourself saying a bunch of positive affirmations and words and play it on repeat while you sleep. It doesn't have to be a perfect speech or studio-level quality. The point here is to reprogram your subconscious mind for the better.

Let's say you want to be more courageous and wealthier. You can record yourself saying things like, *"Courage. I am courageous. I embody courage. Wealth. I am wealthy. I am abundant. Abundance is my natural state. I am courageous. Abundance."*

When in doubt, just say the word you want to embody (or similar words), as well as "I am" + those words.

Just roll with it. Don't be afraid to repeat yourself, or to just say one word and then pause. Remember, the goal here is to reprogram your subconscious mind with those qualities you're speaking of.

You can also leverage this same phenomenon of "subconscious planting" during meditation....

Reprogramming Via Meditation

Meditation is another way of getting your brainwaves into theta.

I like to define meditation as simply, "the practice of building awareness."

Meditation helps you become aware of your thoughts and emotions. It helps you become fully present in the moment.

Meditation comes with a list of benefits that would take another entire book to list out. There's a reason why everyone from spiritual seekers, to psychologists, to high-performing athletes and entrepreneurs are all getting into meditation. It literally enhances every aspect of your life.

For our purposes here, we're going to focus on meditation as a tool of replanting new beliefs in your subconscious mind.

When you relax, both your body and mind, your brainwaves transition from beta, to alpha, then to theta brainwaves. This is the process of meditation.

If you simply sit down, close your eyes, take some deep breaths and observe, you naturally go through this shift in brainwave states over the course of a few minutes.

Once you're in theta, your subconscious mind is primed for reprogramming. How do you know you're primed for reprogramming? You will feel really relaxed and your thoughts will be fading.

From here, you can repeat anything you want to yourself. You do it the same way as the "subconscious planting" when you're falling asleep, it's just that you're in meditation.

Meditation comes with so many benefits, it's almost ridiculous. It literally enhances everything in life.

That's why, if I were to pick one practice from this book to do every single day, that would create the biggest impact in your life, it would be meditation.

Meditation weaves together everything we've discussed so far, from self-inquiry, to awareness of thoughts and emotions, to reprogramming your subconscious mind. And meditation doesn't have to be long or complicated to be beneficial. It can actually be really quick and simple.

If you want to reprogram your subconscious mind with meditation (and experience all of the other benefits too), I have a meditation recommendation for you in the "Practice Sheet" section in the back of the book.

Reprogramming Via Habituation

Reprogramming your subconscious mind with habituation requires consistency. This includes repetitively upgrading your thoughts, your words and your habits.

Over time, this upgrades your subconscious programming (though the exact time frame depends on the person and the activity).

Think about habituation as re-planting your garden one seed at a time. Every thought makes a little difference.

This requires awareness, vigilance and consistency with your thoughts. Whenever you notice an unhelpful thought, "weed it out" by replacing it with something more helpful. This practice might seem tedious, but it's a surefire way to completely upgrade your life.

In addition to being the "guardian at the gate" of your mind and thoughts, there are two even easier ways to reprogram your subconscious mind via habituation...

- Upgrade your "information diet" (all of the information and content you consume)
- Surround yourself with the right people

Diet isn't just the food we eat. The information we take in is also a form of diet. This is common sense. But for whatever reason, most people aren't mindful of the information they consume.

Think about it this way. If all you did was watch horror movies 24/7, your life would have a lot more fear and paranoia. If all you did was watch the news all day, you would think everyone you see is a potential criminal and there's a terrorist around every corner. Combine this with the fact that when you watch something (and sometimes even with reading), you're in a semi-hypnotic state. That's a mainline to your subconsciousness.

So if you want your life to be better, it's a good idea to upgrade your information diet. Only consume helpful information. If you're clear on who you are, your purpose here, and your goals, then it's easy to prioritize helpful information. But if you're lost, and don't care that you're mindlessly imprisoning yourself, you're only going to fortify your self-made prison.

Get in tune with what you want out of life, and make sure your information diet aligns with it. When you do this, you'll find your life improving naturally.

The other one is surrounding yourself with the right people.

Invest time with people who embody the qualities you want. If you want to become wealthier, surround yourself with wealthier people. If you want to be a better writer, befriend some writers. If you want to be happier, surround yourself with happy people. If you want to laugh more, surround yourself with funny people.

You'll not only learn from them, but you'll subconsciously pick up on their behaviors, beliefs, mannerisms, word choices, body language...etc. This will all help you in creating more of that in your life.

Check the people around you. Are they embodying the life you want? If not, it's time to make some changes.

Reprogramming Via Peak Experiences

The last form of subconscious reprogramming is through peak experiences.

As explained before, these are the moments that create a big shift in your perception and life, almost instantaneously.

With peak experiences, you don't have to be as specific when it comes to reprogramming. For example, if someone who lived in the inner city their whole life hiked a mountain for the first time, it would be a paradigm-shifting experience for them. It would reprogram their subconscious mind in a lot of different ways: Belief in themselves, appreciation for nature, a sense of awe, being more present and mindful, a feeling of being connected with all of existence...etc.

Reprogramming with peak experiences comes down to two things:

1. Write a bucket list
2. Do the things on that list

A bucket list is a list of the things you want to do before you die. The kind of things that would be peak experiences for you. And of course, doing them will change your life in major ways.

You can hone in on some general programs to upgrade with peak experiences.

Here are some peak experiences you can create if, for example, you want to improve your relationship with money:
- Give away a sum of money that triggers a little anxiety - This will create a peak experience of giving for you.
- Celebrate any bit of money that comes to you - If you get a paycheck, look at it, put on your favorite song and dance in celebration.
- You can even visualize receiving a large sum of money. Really feel it and celebrate it to make the visualization a peak experience.

If you want more happiness, do something that makes you happy. Let's say you like watching live music. Commit to watching a live show within the next week.

If you want more peace, treat yourself to some self-care and really cherish it (a massage, a bath...etc.). Even something as simple as a nice hot shower can be an amazing experience if you truly appreciate it.

Honing Your Vision

As you begin to upgrade your programming, you allow yourself to step into greater and greater visions.

Clarity comes from a few things:
- Truly knowing what does and doesn't align with the best version of yourself
- Learning to prioritize and focus
- The ability to zoom out your perspective and see the bigger picture
- Honing your intuition

When you know what's in alignment with the best version of yourself, clarity naturally emerges. Remember those three qualities the best version of yourself would embody? Go back to those, use them as guideposts, and more clarity will come to you in all aspects of life.

This also leads to prioritization. When you know what's important and what's distraction or addiction, it's easy to prioritize and focus. When you learn to prioritize what's truly important in life, and focus on that, clarity follows.

Clarity also comes from the ability to see the bigger picture. Most people are so fixated on the "struggles" of daily life that they never let themselves see the big picture. When you allow yourself to zoom out and play with different ways of viewing your life and the world, you gain more clarity.

Play with your lens of perception. Allow yourself to "zoom out" from the grind of daily life and view your whole life at once. Even look at your life in the scope of an even greater reality. Then hold whatever you want more clarity with up to that big picture. Does it fit in? How does it fit in? How does it fit in if you zoom out even more? How does it fit in if you start to narrow that picture?

This simple practice of "widening your lens of perception" can bring you the kind of clarity and insight you've been searching for your whole life in an instant.

Another way to more clarity is to hone your intuition.

Intuition is a sense of inner knowing that can't be explained logically or rationally. Sometimes intuition is a subtle voice. Sometimes intuition comes from feelings. Sometimes intuition is accessed by signs and "strangely improbable coincidences" (called "synchronicities").

<u>**How do you hone your intuition?**</u>
1. **Becoming more aware of your feelings and thoughts**
2. **Acting on and trusting your intuition with little things**

It's really simple. But it requires consistency to cultivate.

The blunt truth about intuition: You probably won't have any earth-shattering "psychic" moments (especially in the beginning), but you will experience subtle whispers, signs and hints. To build your intuition, pay attention to those subtle bits of guidance until they become bigger and bigger.

Awareness is a major theme here. The more aware you are of your thoughts and feelings, the more you gain the ability to discern between your ego's programmed ramblings and the subtle whispers of intuition.

The surefire way to cultivate your intuition is through meditation. Meditation creates a "baseline" environment to practice observing your thoughts, helping you gain the ability to detect subtle intuitive hints.

If you want to leverage the power of meditation, check out my recommendation for you in the "Practice Sheet" section in the back of the book.

Everything we've discussed so far in this book is helping you create more clarity in your life. Clarity isn't the only benefit of course, but even now, clarity is forming - little by little - around your vision and your life.

Clarity isn't a "once and done" state. It's something that comes with continuous refinement. This process of refinement is intertwined with your life journey at large.

Now we'll continue to refine your new life...

What Are You Serving?

To fully let down your guard, you must fully be a guardian.

Service to small self (persona/ego) is a tempting trap. "I'm Stephanie. I'm an accountant. I'm an American. I'm a democrat. I'm an introvert...etc." As we went over before, those are all labels and boxes, not your true self.

Service to your true Self (Pure Awareness or Pure Love) is freedom.

When you're of service to your persona, you're automatically blocked, because you're of service to a box. When you're of service to Love, how can there be blocks? Love is infinite.

With everything you do, ask yourself, "What am I serving?" With the big picture of your life, ask yourself, "What am I serving?"

Remember, it's so easy to deceive ourselves. As the theoretical physicist Richard Feynman famously said, "The first principle is that you must not fool yourself and you are the easiest person to fool."

For example, many religious people will claim they're serving God, when they're really serving their fear of death, their fear of the unknown, their desire to fit in, their fear of responsibility, their fear of their own power...etc.

With several things I created, I thought I was serving people's spiritual growth, but I was also serving my desire to be seen as wise and accomplished. And this reduced the potency of my message.

What you're serving is what you're feeding, and what you're limiting yourself to. If you're serving a fear, guess what you're limiting your experience to? Fear.

If you're serving conflict, guess what you're limiting your experience to? Conflict.

It's common sense. But we deceive ourselves into missing the obvious.

That's why it's key to serve something beyond your ego persona. Something that is expansive and for the greater good of all. When you do this, everyone benefits, including yourself.

Now let's talk about releasing more shackles of the ego persona.

Let Go & Flow

From pure awareness, all is accepted with compassion. There is no resistance.

If there are great people around you, accept them with compassion and flow forward. If there aren't great people around you, accept them with compassion and flow forward. If there is no one around you, accept it with compassion and flow forward.

No judgment. No resistance. Just gratitude and compassion.

Be open to any possibility, meeting every moment with gratitude and compassion. And remember that every situation is temporary.

The "good" things are temporary. The "bad" things are temporary. Either way, meet it with gratitude as it passes through your reality. This shift alone can change everything for you.

Here's the big kicker. When you stop resisting everything, things just start unfolding in a magical way in your life.

This is so empowering. Instead of getting thrown off by everything that doesn't go your way, you let it slide past you, as you continue on your journey.

You know who you really are (pure awareness). You know what's important. You know the direction you're moving in.

From this place, you can choose to let go of everything that doesn't align with that. No overreacting. No clinging. No fixating on it over and over in your head.

If someone is acting rude, you're aware enough to not react. You choose to remove yourself from the situation, calmly ask them to stop, or simply ignore them.

The big win here is that you don't get yourself "stuck" by reacting to every annoyance around you. With your newfound clarity, you flow around every obstacle.

"Empty your mind, be formless, shapeless — like water. Now you put water in a cup, it becomes the cup; You put water into a bottle it becomes the bottle; You put it in a teapot it becomes the teapot. Now water can flow or it can crash. Be water, my friend."
~ Bruce Lee

You're Not Alone

You're unique, but you're not alone.

You might feel lost, but you're not alone.

You don't have to be all lovey-dovey with everyone you meet, but emotionally isolating yourself only creates more pain and suffering.

When you go within, into pure awareness, it's the same pure awareness within me. It's the same pure awareness within everyone. It's the same pure awareness underneath everything.

When you tune into pure awareness, you're actually one with the essence of everything. You only feel lonely when you're lost in your thoughts.

The loneliest I've ever felt in my life was one time when I was on the subway in New York City. I remember it so distinctly. I was surrounded by people, yet I felt so painfully lonely. All because I was working at a job I hated, I was hungover, and I was lost in the anxious thoughts of my monkey mind.

If you believe you're alone, you create loneliness.

And guess what? There's no need to create that.

You are the creator of YOUR reality. That means you're only a victim if you believe you're a victim.

This is your invitation to step into the driver's seat of your own life.

Are you ready to completely upgrade your world? If so, move forward.

If not, pause for a moment... And feel into the program telling you that you need to play small, to stay limited, to be a victim. See it fully, with pure awareness, until it naturally dissolves.

Now bring this upgraded version of yourself to the next chapter...

Chapter 11: Upgrading Your Relationships

Main Question:
Am I Creating Win-Win Relationships with Other People, or Creating More Difficulty in the World?

You're not an island.

You can't exist without other people.

Even if you live alone in a cabin in the woods, where do you get your food? If you grow it all yourself, who taught you? Who built your house? If you did, who taught you how to build it?

There's no way to completely separate ourselves from other people. And there's no way to separate ourselves from relationships in general, because everything is a relationship (your relationship with yourself, your relationship with a situation, your relationship with anything you own, your relationship with other people…etc.).

So it's in your best interest to upgrade your "relationship with relationships." (see what I did there?)

Here's a major point… **Life is a lot better when you have harmonious relationships.**

Now I'm not saying you need to be a social butterfly and be around people 24/7.

Not at all. I prefer being alone most of the time. But not all the time. There are some key relationships in my life that I nurture, and they make my life a lot more enjoyable.

Even though everything in your experience is a relationship, we're focusing on relationships with other people here. The cool thing is that what you've read so far helps you create a better relationship with yourself, automatically boosting your ability to upgrade your other relationships.

It all starts with you. Like Ziggy Marley said, *"I can't make you happy, unless I am."*

This chapter will help you upgrade your relationships, making life better for yourself and everyone you encounter.

There are some simple keys to relationships:
- Seeing everyone as a mirror of you
- Seeing their "best self"
- Honesty
- Compassion
- Balance with giving and receiving
- Creating win-win scenarios

Now let's dive into each...

Seeing Everyone as A Mirror of You

I like practical perspectives.

One of my favorites is to view everyone as a mirror of myself.

Here's what that means. Everyone you encounter in your life represents something going on internally within you.

Many people will say this is literally true. But I'm not going to try to prove that to you. I'm just inviting you to use this perspective, because it will change your life.

With every situation with people in your life, ask yourself, "What is it within me that is drawing this experience into my life?"

It's usually either something that you're carrying within (and are afraid to look at), or something you judge and resist.

Let's get into some examples...

If your significant other is angry all the time, ask yourself what it is within you that is drawing in this experience of anger? It might be showing you your own anger. It might be repressed anger that you have. It might be that you judge anger a lot. It might be that you're afraid of anger, and you're being called to face your fear.

Whatever it is, look within and be 100% honest with yourself.

If your best friend is depressed, ask yourself what it represents within you. Are you secretly depressed? Do you judge depressed people as weak? Are you afraid of falling into depression? Again, take an honest look within.

If your friend is always late, look within. Are you always late? Or do you hold yourself to such a high standard around being on time that you judge yourself whenever you're late? And if you judge yourself for this, you're obviously going to judge everyone else too.

With every situation in life, you can find a lesson in it and use it to fuel your growth.

This "mirror perspective" also helps you become more responsible and empowered. There's no one to blame when you're always asking, "What does this represent within me?"

When you apply this perspective and take full responsibility, there's no excuses.

If you say, "They did that, so I'm mad." It's an excuse and a way of giving your power away to someone else. I mean, c'mon, are you really letting other people or situations determine your emotional state? Or do you take responsibility for your world?

I get it... It's easier to blame everything on someone else. But if you keep doing that, you give away your responsibility for your inner environment and you'll always be a victim.

View everyone as a mirror of your internal state, find the lesson in it and take back your power. You're the master of your reality, not a victim of circumstance.

Seeing Their Best Self

What default stories come into your mind when you think of someone?

Are you focusing on their faults? Or are you focusing on their best self?

Most of us automatically zero-in on faults. As soon as someone comes up in our mind or in conversation, we think "ugh" or say, "yeah, but (insert criticism)."

Let's use examples of two people...

Person 1: Is there someone whose brilliance you see fully? Someone who you love without resistance?

What does it feel like? What kind of thoughts pop up around this person?

Person 2: Is there someone who you always see their faults? Someone who you have a lot of resistance towards?

Try taking those feelings and thoughts about Person 1 and applying them to Person 2. This could be in that way you think about them, how you talk to them or how you act towards them.

Do this whenever you think of them. Continuously replace the judgment with loving thoughts, until the loving thoughts become your default thoughts towards them.

Focus on their best self, not their hang-ups. This will completely upgrade any relationship.

It doesn't mean being naive. It doesn't mean allowing yourself to get taken advantage of.

You can be aware of their flaws and hang-ups. But criticizing them only creates more resistance. And you can love them while still holding boundaries and not letting yourself get taken advantage of. You will find this balance in every relationship as you apply these tools.

This technique simply means that you feed their best self - not their "problems" or character flaws - while still being aware enough to not subject yourself to any harm or manipulation.

Honesty

Honesty is absolutely crucial for harmonious, balanced relationships.

First of all though, you need to learn how to be honest with yourself. If you can't be honest with yourself, you can't be honest with anyone else.

For example, if something someone did bothers you, you need to admit it to yourself first. Don't sweep it under the rug. Don't pretend like you're not bothered, when you really are. Then, after you get honest with yourself, you can communicate that to the other person. You don't need to lash out or be mean. You can calmly and clearly say that you were bothered.

With honesty, it's important that you deliver it without negative emotions behind it. If you say something honest with resentment, most people are going to react, even if it's true.

That's why it's paramount to stay centered and non-reactive when giving or receiving honest communication.

It's surprising how many "sensitive topics" two non-reactive people can talk about. It's also surprising how two reactive people can't communicate anything honestly without it turning into a big fiasco.

If you're not mature enough to "go there" (to say what needs to be said) while being grounded and centered, little lies, and things left unsaid are going to add up and make any relationship toxic.

A classic example of this is a husband who watches TV every night to "relax." His wife doesn't like it. She would rather they spend time with each other and just talk. But she's scared to speak her truth, so she represses what she feels every day. Then, every time they're both irritated, she throws it in his face, saying, "You're always watching TV and you don't even care about me!"

But if she was able to communicate her needs on a daily basis (without judging or attacking him), it gives him the opportunity to change. And unless he has crazy anger problems, he'll be receptive to hear the clear, balanced communication of her needs.

It comes down to this. Have the courage to say what needs to be said, and speak it from a place of compassion and non-judgment.

Honesty also comes with a balance that is unique to every situation. It's impossible to narrate every moment of your life, or every thought you've ever had. So you need to say what's relevant and important. But when most people "filter for relevancy" they twist things to fit their story. This is why it's crucial to be honest with yourself and in full integrity. If not, you trap yourself in your own web of lies.

Honesty is a breath of fresh air. Have the courage to clear the air, both within yourself and your relationships. Trust me, it makes everything a lot easier, enjoyable and more harmonious.

Compassion

Compassion is the ability to put yourself in someone else's shoes and show them love.

As humans, especially in modern Western society, we get caught up in our own ego-driven drama. When this is happening, we fall into the mode of protecting ourselves, not being able to see past the walls of our own delusion.

Have you ever noticed that when you're pissed off, you don't care at all about the well-being of others? You're just preoccupied with anger, judgment and self-protection. It might even be to the point where you would rather hurt others than help them, because you're so "possessed" by anger.

Then there's the other side of the coin. Have you ever been so happy that you naturally spread happiness to everyone you meet, without even really trying? Ah, we're onto something now.

This is because there's no drama going on within. You're clear, so you can see clearly. When you can see clearly, you truly see other people. And when you truly see other people, you naturally exude compassion.

I don't think compassion is something you have to force or try to do. You just need to get yourself together, and compassion naturally emerges.

So I'm not telling you how to be compassionate. I'm saying to take responsibility for your inner world, be a better person, and you will automatically be compassionate.

It's a win-win. You feel great, and you help other people feel great. But if you're caught up in your own ego-centric drama, it's a lose-lose. You're miserable and you spread your misery around to everyone else. And why would anyone consciously choose that? Well, no one would, because it's unconscious behavior.

Bring awareness to your inner world and create that win-win. When you look at it that way, it's a no-brainer, right?

Balance with Giving & Receiving

What's a relationship where you give all the time, without receiving? It's exhausting and draining.

What's a relationship where you receive all the time, without giving? Well, you're an egotistical parasite.

Think about breathing. If you only exhale, it doesn't work out well. If you only inhale, it doesn't work out well either. Life thrives in an ever-flowing movement of giving and receiving.

Relationships thrive on a balance of giving and receiving too.

And no, you don't need to track giving and receiving like it's some kind of balance sheet. That just blocks the fun and spontaneity of it all.

Giving and receiving in healthy relationships are an ebb and flow. You give when you're inspired to give, because you want to give to that person, not because you have to.

With every relationship, focus on giving. If you focus on receiving, you're like a spoiled kid always expecting their parents to buy them something, and constantly disappointed when your ridiculous expectations aren't met.

Focus on giving, and remember that giving comes in many forms. Here are some ideas…
- Quality time
- Truly listening
- Genuinely asking how they're doing
- Asking, "How can I help?"
- Buying a gift
- Doing a favor

- Cleaning for them
- Writing a letter
- Sending a card
- Taking them out for a meal
- Cooking them a meal
- Giving a genuine compliment
- Saying "thank you"
- Sharing an idea that might help them
- Giving them a book (like this one, *hint-hint*)

What forms of giving feel good for you? Start there.

In every relationship, ask yourself this question...
"How can I give in a way that makes their life better AND feels good for me?"

Asking that simple question, and following through with it, will automatically make every relationship in your life a lot better.

Creating Win-Win Scenarios

Are you against the people you interact with? Or do you believe you're all on the same team?

If you resist people, and think they're against you, or you're against them, guess what you create in your life? Conflict, enemies, stress, drama...etc. I don't know about you, but I definitely don't want any more of that stuff in my life.

So why do we create that? There are two false beliefs that create resistance and conflict in all relationships:
1. **Thinking one person has to lose for the other to win**
2. **Judging people for not acting the way you want them to act**

To harmonize your relationships and transcend all of the conflict and drama, you need a win-win mentality.

In every interaction, think, "How can I create a win-win here?"

Hint: Win-win situations are always possible, if you can see past your own limitations.

We've been so conditioned to accept the "win-lose" paradigm; "They need to lose for me to win." Honestly, it's short-sighted, unproductive and limiting.

Here's another way to look at it… All battles are "lose-lose". If you think about it, if you're engaged in conflict or drama, it's not fun.

Does anyone set a goal of arguing for an hour? Of course not. And even if you "win" an argument, congratulations, you just spent an hour in conflict and drama to boost your ego.

Again, always think, "win-win."

Some people say that this happens through compromise. But that isn't how you create win-win scenarios.

You create win-win scenarios through co-creation. This means that you come together as a team to co-create situations with people, from the initial idea to the end result. It's a shared vision.

Let's say you and a friend want to meet for lunch. You really want a sandwich, and they really want to go somewhere close to them. So you brainstorm a place closer to them that has good sandwiches. You let the idea evolve as you communicate with them, and as a result, there's a win-win. You get your sandwich and they don't have to go far from their home.

Here's another example. My girlfriend and I need a quiet, peaceful space to record videos in our house. And her teenage son wants a place where he can hang out and listen to music. So we let him turn our garage into his hangout spot. The idea came about as we were all talking about what we wanted. That's a win-win through co-creation. We get our quiet, peaceful space, and he gets his hangout spot.

The other false belief that creates resistance and conflict is judgment.

We all judge each other.

We think we know best and project that onto everyone else.

If someone doesn't do something your way, they're wrong. If someone doesn't value the same things as you, they're wrong.

This kind of judgment only creates resistance between you and other people.

Live and let live, baby.

And if someone is trying to cause harm to you, remove yourself from the situation. Or, if it's a bit complicated, at least take a step towards getting out of the situation.

But if you judge people as "wrong", all you're doing is creating conflict and drama in your own life. And really, no one wants that.

Live Every Interaction Like It's Your Last

Here's a perspective that will completely transform your life…

Live every interaction like it's your last.

With every interaction you have, treat it like it's your last interaction with that person.

Life is impermanent. Every moment is fleeting. Tomorrow isn't promised.

Honestly, any interaction could be your last. Maybe you won't be here tomorrow, or maybe the other person won't be.

This isn't to be morbid or scare you. The perspective of "living every interaction like it's your last" allows you to fully cherish every moment.

The more you truly realize how impermanent life is, the more you appreciate it.

Even if someone's mad at you, how would you treat them if you knew it was the last time you would see them? You would show them compassion, or at the very least not react to their anger and get yourself all worked up.

Live every interaction like it's your last.

You don't need to be dramatic about it, or walk around crying that anyone could die tomorrow. It's more about cherishing and appreciating every moment.

Speak from your heart, tell that person you love them, let go of negativity, express your creativity.

If you live life treating every interaction like it's your last, your life will be pure magic. I mean, how could your life NOT be magical? It really forces you to focus on what's actually important in life, and let go of the trivial little hang ups.

When you live every interaction like it's your last, you live fully. No regrets. No drama. Just pure compassionate bliss.

Chapter 12: You 2.0

Main Question:
How Would the Best Version of Myself Think, Feel and Live?

This is your activation.

Life will never be the same.

YOU will never be the same.

And that's amazing.

The only constant is change. Everything changes, no matter what.

With the tools shared in this book, you have the ability to consciously change. You can now choose to upgrade your life, instead of being subject to changes from external forces. With your newfound awareness, you now hold the power of choice.

Let's recap quickly…

It all starts with the core question, "Who am I?" The only real answer is "I am," or "pure awareness."

From here, bring awareness to your thoughts and emotions. What thoughts are you having right now? What emotions are you feeling right now?

Then, with this awareness, you can acquaint more with the real you. You can reveal so much by asking yourself, "What is driving me?" in various situations.

Recognize your superpower of choice. In every moment, ask yourself, "Do I have a choice right now?" It's a trick question, because you always have a choice. Even saying you don't is a choice. Choice is your superpower to create your best life.

The big ship of your life has a small rudder. That rudder is your power of choice. If you make one small shift, it creates massive change over time. So ask yourself, "What is one little shift I can make today?"

Like Lao Tzu said, "A journey of a thousand miles begins with a single step." If you take one small step every day, it amounts to BIG things before you know it. What is one small step you can take every day to move in a positive direction?

As you move, let go of your self-imposed limitations and embrace all possibility. Ask yourself, "What conditions am I placing on my life?"

From here, choose to reprogram your subconscious mind with upgraded beliefs. Ask yourself, "What is an affirming belief I want to reprogram my mind with?" And start seeding, whether it's as you go to sleep, during meditation or another subconscious reprogramming technique.

You're not alone. And you're not an island. You have the opportunity to have the best relationships ever in your life. Are you creating win-win relationships with other people, or creating more difficulty in the world?

Finally, You 2.0 emerges. How would the best version of myself think, feel and live? Get clear on this, visualize it, feel it, and start embodying it every day. You already have everything you need.

You are now a new you. Your essence, pure awareness, is still the same. But now you have the opportunity to bring it all the way through into your daily life. It's a rebirth of everything you thought you were, into everything you are.

When you close this book, commit to embodying this rebirth.

Remember your true self, pure awareness, the "I Am" presence. From here and now, anything is possible.

Look within, and I'll meet you there.

Step forward into infinite possibility.

Sending you deep love and many blessings along your journey.

Wholeheartedly,
Stephen Parato

Main Questions from Each Chapter

Come back to these questions every day for greater insight and clarity

1. Who am I?

2. What thoughts am I having right now?

3. What emotions am I feeling right now?

4. What is driving me?

5. Do I have a choice right now?

6. What is one little shift I can make today?

7. What is one small step I can take every day to move in a positive direction?

8. Why am I here?

9. What conditions am I placing on my life?

10. What is an affirming belief I want to reprogram my mind with?

11. Am I creating win-win relationships with other people, or creating more difficulty in the world?

12. How would the best version of myself think, feel and live?

*You can download these questions at stephenparato.com/abookforyou

Practice Sheet

This is your practice sheet, to help you apply and integrate everything discussed in this book.

You don't have to apply these all at once. No need to overwhelm yourself.

Here are some recommended approaches…
1. **Go through these one at a time, applying each as recommended**
2. **Pick one practice that excites you, focus on that, then repeat with another practice that excites you**
3. **When in doubt, start with meditation (it enhances everything else)**

Come back to this practice sheet as often as you feel. These practices are all simple, yet incredibly powerful.

You can also download this sheet at stephenparato.com/abookforyou

Practice 1: Who Am I?
Pause, take a few deep breaths and ask yourself:
- Who is the thinker of my thoughts?
- Who is the observer of the thinker of my thoughts?

Frequency: AMAP*

AMAP = As Much As Possible

Practice 2: Watch Your Thoughts
- Bring awareness to your thoughts
- Just watch (don't judge or resist)

The more often you observe your thoughts, the better. Create a tally for yourself with this. Come up with a reward for yourself for doing this 10 times per day for a week.

Frequency: AMAP

Practice 3: Express Your Emotions in A Healthy Way

- Bring awareness to your emotional state
- What specific emotion are you experiencing?
- If you feel off or imbalanced, express yourself in a healthy way (don't suppress or take it out on other people)

Frequency: AMAP

Practice 4: Choice Shifting

- Pick a situation in your life that you want to change for the better
- What's a simple mental shift that would help?
- How would your best self view this situation?
- What's a daily action that you can take to improve this situation?

Frequency: Whenever you feel like a situation is limiting you

Practice 5: Purpose
- Pick one life purpose question
- Journal your response to it
- Do this with as many questions as you feel

Frequency: Once per question, on a daily basis.

Life Purpose Questions:
- What excites me?
- What kind of ideas come to me in the shower?
- What kind of things do people always ask me about?
- What topics do I regularly read about?
- During which experiences in my life have I felt the most alive?
- What unique interests, or abilities, did I have as a young child?
- What would I be doing if money were no object?
- What would I be doing if I absolutely, 100%, did not care about what other people think?
- What is on my bucket list?
- What topics can I blend together to create my own unique niche?

- If I were to write a short (1-2 sentence) "About Me", describing the ideal version of myself, what would it be?
- What causes do I strongly believe in, or connect with?
- What activities make me lose track of time?
- If I had to teach something, what would I teach?
- What challenges or obstacles have I overcome in life?

You can access my mini-book about this (20 Questions to Reveal Your Life's Purpose) via the resources page for this book: stephenparato.com/abookforyou

Practice 6: Clear Vision
- What's a vision or goal you have for your life?
- Ask yourself, "Is this mine?" (Or is it something you picked up from your parents, family, school, media, celebrities, or society in general?)
- If it's not yours, let go
- Imagine the vision happening right now: Does it feel expansive? If not, let go.
- Is this vision closer to your best, most loving self? If not, let go.
- If it passed through all of those filters, sit and envision it.
- Create a daily action plan that brings you in the direction of this vision
- Keep an eye out for signs, and allow yourself to shift direction if need be

Frequency: Whenever you need clear direction in your life

Practice 7: Meditation

As mentioned several times, meditation creates a foundation for all of this.

Meditation helps you…
- Create mental and emotional mastery
- Get in tune with your true self
- Find your power of choice
- Get clearer on your real purpose
- Discern between your ego's wants and your soul's vision
- Thoroughly embrace and in-joy every moment, no matter the circumstance

Here's the thing with meditation though… Everyone knows it's beneficial, but very few people actually meditate on a regular basis.

You only get the benefits of meditation when you make it a regular practice.

That's why I created the simplest way to cultivate a regular meditation practice, while taking a deeper dive into the concepts in this book. And if you already meditate, it's the simplest way to deepen your meditation practice.

You can access it via the resources page for this book → stephenparato.com/abookforyou

Practice 8: Alien Thought Experiment

Imagine yourself as an alien who just teleported into your body right now.

You have no attachment to human culture or history. You look around and see the world from a neutral perspective. Your mental and emotional awareness is at the peak of what you can imagine.

What would you do with the rest of your life? What would you work towards? What kind of impact would you make? How would you go about your day?

Frequency: Whenever your perspective seems stale, stagnant or stuck.

Practice 9: The 3 Qualities of Your Best Self

Write down 3 qualities that your best self would embody. Explain each quality as specifically as possible.

Frequency: Once per month (or as often as you feel)

Practice 10: Subconscious Reprogramming Around Sleep

Plant a positive seed in your mind as you drift into sleep every night, and as the first thing you think of when you wake up. This can be a word, phrase or affirmation.

Frequency: Every time you fall asleep, and every time you wake up

Try this out for a week. If you like it, great. If not, try listening to an audio recording.

Practice 11: Subconscious Reprogramming Via Habituation

- Bring awareness to your thoughts as often as possible
- Weed out unhelpful thoughts by replacing each with a more helpful thought
- Invest time with people who embody what you want to embody
- Upgrade your information diet

Frequency: AMAP

Practice 12: Subconscious Reprogramming with Super-Learning

- Create a bucket list
- Complete one item this week

Check off a bucket list item every week moving forward (even if it's something small).

Frequency: Every week

Practice 13: Creating Win-Win Scenarios

With every interaction ask yourself, "How can I create a win-win here?" Write down your ideas, or even ask the people you're with to come up with ideas together. Then apply it.

Frequency: Every time you do something with someone

Spread the Love

If you found value in this book, please spread the love in any way you can.

Here are some ideas:
- Buy this book for a friend or family member
- Give away copies to people who would benefit from these messages
- Tell your network about this book and the wisdom within it

<u>If you found value in this book, please leave a review online</u>. This is an easy way to help this book reach more people.

Let us live with freedom and empowerment. Let us be lighthouses in this world. And in being so, we naturally inspire others as well.

About the Author

Stephen Parato is a writer, creativity wizard, meditation guide, ancient wisdom keeper and founder of FeelinGoodFeelinGreat.com.

His passion is to share tools that spark empowerment, create mindfulness in daily life, and help you tap into your creative genius.

Stephen is the author of 20+ books and several online courses, which can be found through his websites:

- StephenParato.com
- FeelinGoodFeelinGreat.com
- WholeHeartEmbodiment.com

www.ingramcontent.com/pod-product-compliance
Lightning Source LLC
Chambersburg PA
CBHW022115040426
42450CB00006B/707